# Smart Money Stupid Money

How small changes in your daily life can secure your future.

Mike Swedenberg

Copyright © 2017 James Michael Swedenberg

All rights reserved. No part of this publication may be reproduced, distributed, or transmitted in any form or by any means, including photocopying, recording, or other electronic or mechanical methods, without the prior written permission of the publisher, except in the case of brief quotations embodied in critical reviews and certain other noncommercial uses permitted by copyright law. For permission requests, write to the Author, addressed "Attention: Permissions Coordinator," at mike@swedenberg.com

Brand names, logos and trademarks used herein are the property of their respective owners. This listing of any company, blog, website, publisher or their logos is not intended to imply any endorsement or direct affiliation with this publication.

The information contained herein is on an "as is" basis, without warranties or conditions of any kind, either express or implied, including, without limitation, any warranties or conditions of title, non-infringement, merchantability, or fitness for a particular purpose. You agree that you will not rely on and are solely responsible for determining the appropriateness of using the information provided in this book and assume any risks associated with doing so.

ISBN-13: 978-1540423764

ISBN-10: 154042376X

# DEDICATION

To my mother who taught me the value of money

# Contents

Spend the Principle and it's Gone Forever ................................................. 6

Never Start Any Business Unless… ........................................................ 10

Rule of 72 ................................................................................................ 20

Pay yourself first ..................................................................................... 30

Lease or Purchase a Car .......................................................................... 30

Poverty is a State of Mind ....................................................................... 47

Never Let Anyone Manage Your Money ............................................... 51

More Case Studies of Stupid Money ...................................................... 54

Timeshare ................................................................................................ 57

Waiting for Politicians to Fix Your Problems ........................................ 59

Am I guilty of Stupid Money? ................................................................ 62

In Conclusion .......................................................................................... 65

ABOUT THE AUTHOR ........................................................................ 66

# Disclaimer

The author is not a Certified Financial Planner, Tax Attorney or a Certified Public Accountant. The information provided is a summary of his lifelong learning, education and experiences.

The advice provided in this book and eBook is general advice only. It has been prepared without taking into account your objectives, financial situation or needs. Before acting on this advice you should consider the appropriateness of the advice, having regard to your own objectives, financial situation and needs. If any products are detailed in this book or eBook, you should obtain a Product Disclosure Statement relating to the products and consider its contents before making any decisions. Where quoted, past performance is not indicative of future performance.

James Michael Swedenberg disclaims all and any guarantees, undertakings and warranties, expressed or implied, and shall not be liable for any loss or damage whatsoever (including human or computer error, negligent or otherwise, or incidental or consequential loss or damage) arising out of or in connection with any use or reliance on the information or advice on this site. The reader must accept sole responsibility associated with the use of the material here within, irrespective of the purpose for which such use or results are applied. The information on this website is no substitute for financial advice.

Although the author and publisher have made every effort to ensure that the information in this book was correct at press time, the author and publisher do not assume and hereby disclaim any liability to any party for any loss, damage, or disruption caused by errors or omissions, whether such errors or omissions result from negligence, accident, or any other cause.

Consult with a professional advisor before making any financial decisions.

"If money management isn't something you enjoy, consider my perspective. I look at managing my money as if it were a part-time job. The time you spend monitoring your finances will pay off. You can make real money by cutting expenses and earning more interest on savings and investments. I'd challenge you to find a part-time job where you could potentially earn as much money for just an hour or two of your time."
― Laura D. Adams, Money Girl's Smart Moves to Deal with Your Debt

# Introduction

My introduction to the value of money came to me as a child at the age of seven. It was 1958 and I lived in the upper middle-class suburbs of Greenville, South Carolina.

Although my sheltered childhood provided me with my day to day needs, what I really craved was the Hopalong Cassidy six shooter cap gun and holster. It would help me even the odds with my friends that I played Cowboys and Indians with just about every weekend. All I had was a wooden six shooter, a hand me down from my older brother. It didn't shoot anything, not a single cap. My partners laughed when I was running after the bad guys shouting bang bang. There was no popping sound and no long stream of spent caps hanging from my six shooter to prove my contribution to the chase. Worst of all I missed out on that lingering sweet odor of gun powder on my hands. With my waistband serving as a makeshift holster, I tried my best to compete.

My friends' parents had bought them either the state-of-the-art Roy Rogers six shooter, the Mattel Fanner 50 or the Gene Autry 44 Side Shooter. All fine and respectable side-arms but never rising to the level of the Hopalong Cassidy.

Of course the rich kid in the neighborhood had the entire Roy Rogers costume with hat, rifle, double holster, boots, spurs, chaps and what seemed like an endless supply of caps. He always looked like he stepped off the cover of the Sears Roebuck catalogue. Never playing too hard or working up a sweat, he was careful of the warning from his mother not to soil his play clothes. Usually, he would just lean up against a wall and fan his gun at the bad guys but not much else. By comparison, as hard as

I played to make up for the lack of ammo and a decent cap gun, I looked like a tumble weed that just blew into town.

Our bicycles served as our horses and I named mine Topper in honor of Hopalong's stallion. As we roped stray doggies and chased away cattle rustlers, the rich kid coasted along behind doing little more than lending moral support.

My parents were hard working and good providers but an extravagance like a new six shooter, especially a top of the line Hopalong Cassidy, would have to wait at least until my birthday some months away. I needed to arm myself before the next shootout with the cattle rustlers.. Our scout reported they were camped just outside the local playground and were on the move. He reckoned they would strike Saturday morning right after the Lone Ranger TV show ended.

These were anxious times as I weighed my options. My weekly allowance was decent enough, twenty-five cents, which kept me in Sugar Daddies, a monthly Superman comic book and an occasional banana split at the Woolworths Soda Fountain. If memory serves, the price of the gun set was about three dollars. All I had in my piggy bank was seventy-seven cents and even if I saved every penny of my allowance, summer would be over before I could afford it.

On occasion my mother would hire me out to pull weeds at my grandparents, but I never got paid. She called it a "love job." A heart felt thank you, milk and cookies were payment enough in her view.

My friend Jacky owned an older Wyatt Earp Buntline Special that he was willing to let go for fifty cents but the hammer was broken making it impossible to fan, the simulated pearl handle was cracked and the holster was held together with tape and staples. Several of the straps on the cartridge belt were missing making it look like it barely survived the Alamo. To make matters worse, his little sister had drawn stars and rainbows all over the holster with a ball point pen. Imagine showing up at the camp fire with that strapped around your waist. It was a deal killer even when Jacky dropped the price to 35 cents out of consideration he was my best friend.

My only option was to dig into the jar of coins my grandfather gave me, a collection of silver dimes, quarters and a half dollars, some dating back to the 1890s. He gave them to me with the understanding I was not to spend it on candy or junk. He said if I held them into adulthood, they could be valuable. The only exception was an emergency. Well in my mind, being armed with a wooden gun during a cattle rustler raid constituted an emergency on a grand scale.

I waited till I was home alone, poured the jar out on my bed and counted my treasure. It totaled almost twenty-dollars. I took four dollars for the gun and a few boxes of caps. I rode Topper the five miles to Sears and made my purchase. I strapped it on as soon as the lady handed me the receipt and change. I did a quick draw, stared down the top of the barrel admiring the craftsmanship and balance, pulled back the hammer a few times, gave it a quick twirl and dropped it deftly into the holster. On the way home, I stopped the local saloon, also known as the Clock Drive In, for a Pepsi and fries. My problem solved and none the wiser except for my eagle-eyed mother who spotted the gun and holster as soon as I walked into the house.

After explaining my dilemma and the source of the funds, Mother confiscated the gun until I had earned enough to replace the money. She explained the rest of the cash was to be put into a savings account where it would earn interest every month and as long as I didn't make a withdrawal, it would continue to earn interest forever. But if I spent that money, what she called the principal, it was gone forever. Mother explained while sitting in the jar my money earned nothing but in a savings account it would grow and next month the interest would earn interest. Over time my balance would double even if I never put any more money into my account, as long as I didn't touch it.

My eyes widened at the possibilities. How was this possible? Was it even legal? What idiot would pay me to hold my money? If someone asked me to hold their money for a month, I surely wouldn't pay them interest. What was the point? But I believed everything my parents told me and agreed to open an account.

That afternoon, we visited the Savings and Loan where my parents did their banking and opened my own account. The teller patiently counted out sixteen dollars and thirty cents. She dropped the coins in her drawer, examining the dates on some of the dimes, typed something in a book and handed it to me. She said congratulations, you're on the way to being a great saver, or something to that effect. I also received a little pin I could put on my lapel and a handful of coin holders that I could fill with dimes and deposit when full.

As I waited outside the bank for my mother to finish up, I pondered how to come up with the three dollars and fifty cents so I could get my gun and holster out of hock. I wandered over to a row of payphones and checked the coin return for any change. On occasion I had done this whenever I passed a payphone and sometimes found a coin or two a grown-up had left behind. I pulled on the return lever a few times and heard a cascade of falling coins strike the metal bin. I stuck my finger into the slot and pulled out a half dozen coins. My hands trembled as I counted my treasure, three quarters and some dimes. I looked to see if the coast was clear and shoved the loot into my pocket. I checked the other phones and retrieved a few more dimes. Then it hit me, I learned a new source of revenue that didn't require weed pulling. As soon as we returned home, I tossed the money into my piggy bank and started filling the dime holder. I was well on the way, but I decided to keep my discovery to myself.

I mounted Topper and rode off to the shopping mall and everywhere else I know that had a payphone. By the end of the week I had retrieved nearly four dollars. I spread them out on my desk, stacked them into neat plies and summoned my mother. I stood there, pointing to them, beaming with pride and asked for my gun and holster. After she was convinced I was on the up and up, she handed over my shootin' iron much as a sheriff returning a firearm to a cowboy just released from jail. The money was destined for my savings account. I rode out to help my partners fend off the cattle rustlers with my new Hopalong Cassidy six shooter gleaming in the sun.

This was my introduction to the banking system as well. Sometime later I withdrew some money from my account with my mother's permission. I was shocked that they gave me dollar bills and not the original coins I had deposited. I thought they would keep my savings in a separate pile reserved for me. I knew someone made off with my silver coins. It was a shocking lesson along with the mystery of the bank paying me to hold my money.

Until I was old enough to get my first job, I kept my payphone route, fine tuning it to hit the best payers and eliminate the ones that were duds. I made enough that I never again accepted allowance from my parents. By the time I was thirteen, I felt uncool checking phone booths and was old enough to earn money raking lawns and other odd jobs in the neighborhood. I continued to build my savings account and eventually bought my first ten shares of stock at age fourteen.

# Spend the Principle and it's Gone Forever

There is an old adage that if you spend the principal it's gone forever, but if you spend the interest you get more next month. I have made this my hallmark of personal finances.

If you earn a thousand dollars and spend it, you will never see that money again. It will be gone forever. If on the other hand, you invest the money into a CD, savings account or dividend paying stock, you will have a stream of income that will last a lifetime.

**A Case Study in Stupid Money**

A few years ago I worked with a younger man who told me that he once held a waiters' position at a well-known restaurant on Long Island. Twice a week a certain group of men would frequent this restaurant for lunch. They never discussed their business but my coworker assumed they were somehow associated with organized crime. This crew took a liking to my friend and requested his table each time. They proceeded to order almost everything on the menu and a half dozen bottles of expensive wine. The tab often exceeded eight-hundred dollars. They always paid in cash and left my friend a two-hundred dollars cash tip each time. This went on for a year until one day they never showed up again.

I asked my friend what he did with all of the money. He said he lived at home with his folks while going to school and had no expenses except a car payment and his clothes. He took home enough gourmet left-overs from the restaurant that fed his family for several days and that was his contribution to living with his parents. Since he had no idea what to do with the money, he started going to the mall every week and spent the tips on whatever caught his fancy. In no time, his closet was filled with clothes, shoes, jackets and hats, some he said he never wore. He bought bracelets, watches and electronics that sat unopened on his bureau drawer. He admitted that he would stay at the mall until the money was spent even if it meant he bought some perfume for his mom, a power tool for his dad or ate a meal when he really wasn't hungry. Once when he got home from a spree, he realized he had left a bag of new shirts at the register after paying for them. He was to disinterested to make the ten minute drive back to the store and chalked it up as a loss.

I asked if he managed to save any of his salary or tip money and he replied he never had a bank account and the thought never crossed his mind. As a child when he received an allowance or money as a gift, he'd go out and buy something. He had a piggy bank but no one explained what it was used for other than to hold coins. It sat on top of his dresser collecting dust.

At the end of each season, he gave the clothes, with the sales tags still attached, to charity to make room for new arrivals. The electronics were tossed or given away when he realized he had no use for them. Now, ten years older with responsibilities of a family, he regrets never putting money aside. He managed to run up debt buying things he needed for his family. How he wished he had saved some of that windfall.

Why my friend never thought to save some or all of his tip money, we'll never know. Perhaps he had no training in money management. Maybe he thought the gravy train would never end.

**A Case Study in Smart Money**

In 2006, another coworker had received a fifteen-thousand dollar commission check for an exceptional sales quarter. Without hesitation, he deposited it into his brokerage account and bought shares of a pharmaceutical company that paid good dividends. He had the dividends automatically reinvested into buying more shares and after five years he had doubled the original investment. He is another ten years away from retirement and when the time comes he's confident the stock will be worth eighty-thousand dollars. This is based on the dividend reinvestment and the stock growth from fifty dollars to one hundred and twenty-five dollars a share. At that point he will start taking the dividends out as cash, or about four thousand dollars a year for the rest of his life without ever touching the principal. This is above and beyond his 401 k and his other retirement plans including Social Security.

These extremes of these two accounts are exceptions. Who has a wait-staff job that gets four hundred dollars a week in tips from just one party? I have heard of bartenders at trendy spots that can rake it in but for the vast majority of us, it's not possible to find such an opportunity. And not everyone can find a commissioned sales position that can generate huge bonus checks.

How do these examples help you?

Find a way to generate even a small amount of money every week, like a part time job, selling unwanted household items on eBay, used books on Amazon.com or flipping burgers part-time at a fast food joint. Set aside ten hours a week and even at ten dollars an hour you can earn four thousand dollars in income a year dedicated to your life savings. Resist the temptation to spend the money, rather invest it in something in which that you have a comfort level. Start reading the financial pages of the newspaper either in print, online or at the library. Most papers list all of the best CD rates, savings account interest rates in your area. Find the best one and start accumulating wealth,

Interest rates are low now and the stock market is your best option but it requires a certain level of fortitude, research and stamina to invest. If you don't have the time or desire to invest in the market then secured CDs and Bonds are your next best thing. I cannot offer specific recommendations but the information is at your fingertips. Remember if you buy a five year CD with the highest return, then your money will be tied up for five years. Things change and you might want to limit your CDs to one a year term and roll it over the following year at possibly a higher rate. Mutual Funds are another option. Many return ten-percent or more per year.

Mike Swedenberg

# Never Start Any Business Unless…
you have seven years' experience in that business.

I'm a big fan of the reality shows like Jon Taffer's Bar Rescue, Gordon Ramsey's Kitchen Nightmares and Marcus Lemonis' The Profit. Each episode showcases a failing business and how the host comes to the rescue and helps many of their clients repair their businesses and prosper.

One of the common themes of each of the shows is that the owners just fell into their business with no practical experience in that business. I recall one couple who came across a closed bar that was for sale. They thought it would be fun to buy it and see if they could succeed. It didn't take long for the couple to wind up in over their heads and on the brink of losing everything.

It's easy to sit back in the comfort of my home and be Monday morning quarterback but sometimes I have to wonder what these people were thinking. Would they have opened a dental practice and started drilling teeth even though neither one was a dentist? Would they have mortgaged their home and sunk their life savings into a computer network security company even though they barely knew how to turn a computer on? Of course not. But what is it about businesses like restaurants, bars, nail salons and clothing stores that makes folks think they can wing it?

I have my own dream to open the Swedenberg Beer Garden to capitalize on my Scandinavian name. I know I want to open it in Brooklyn in a neighborhood with high foot traffic so I don't have the liability of customers driving after having a few drinks. I know I would allow customers to order take-out from local restaurants so I wouldn't have to deal with a kitchen, chef and all the related problems. I'd charge a small setting fee of two or three dollars to cover the costs of clean up. I know I'd invite local craft brewers in for sampling and special offers. I'd only have one or two large screen TV's for big games without turning it into a generic sports bar. I'd also like to be located near one of the colleges in Brooklyn. I would write a detailed business plan, take some courses to be trained as a sommelier. This would enable me to offer wine along with the beer and I know I don't want to offer hard liquor. I have the resources to do it, a strong back ground in sales, marketing and advertising and even five years working as a bartender.

What is stopping me? I know enough about the business to know I don't know nearly enough to be successful. I don't have a solid seven years' experience in the business nor at my stage in life do I have the time to acquire it. There is so much I need to learn even though a beer garden is just a grown up version of a Kool-Aid stand. The most complicated things would be filling out the liquor license and negotiating the lease.

Instead I have decided to build a small publishing company and produce how to and self-help books like the one you are reading. I have sixteen years' experience in the publishing industry and I'm already off to a good start with twenty titles. Since the only investment I have to make is time, there is no risk. I have a better chance of success doing something I have intimate knowledge of rather than taking a chance on something I know little about but would enjoy far more.

You might ask why not partner with someone with the experience you are lacking. The answer is, I'd work for someone who knew more than me so I could learn. It is in their best interest to train me well. But if I partnered with someone who knew more than me, I'd never be confident he or she was being straight. I'd worry they might be taking advantage of the situation.

I have heard horror stories of that happening and it rarely works out for the lesser experienced partner. A partner who worked the back end of the restaurant cooked the books along with the steaks. The state tax department seized their restaurant and all of the assets for nonpayment of taxes.

Another story of four friends who opened a bar and the one who was responsible for ordering the liquor was skimming off the top. In eight years he'd stolen enough to go out and open his own bar.

Two lifelong friends, one a pharmacist and the other a retailer opened a drug store in Manhattan. The pharmacist began buying expired drug samples from dishonest pharmaceutical representatives and selling them through the store to fill prescriptions. When the DEA caught up with him the retail partner was judged compliance and went to prison along with the pharmacist. His defense didn't get him out of trouble, "I don't know anything about pharmaceuticals or filing prescriptions. I never even met with the drug reps. I had no idea what was happening." He unwittingly shared in the enormous profits without question and at the end of the day, it was his responsibility to be involved.

The adage still stands, "Go into business with your friend and you will lose your friend and your business."

Following are two examples of people pursuing their dreams.

## A Case Study in Stupid Money

An acquaintance we shall call Robert, relayed this story to me some years after the fact. He inherited thirty-thousand dollars from his parents' estate. He wanted to invest in his future and leave his low-pay deadened job. That was smart money thinking. The problem he created is that he chose to open a pizzeria without any experience in the restaurant business save for a part time summer job at a coffee shop when he was a teen.

Robert's only knowledge of pizza was that he liked to eat it. He often waited to pick up his order and watched the pizza maker prepare the pies. It didn't look overly complicated to form the dough, ladle on the sauce and cheese and add toppings. He noted how long the cook left the pies in the oven, how they were sliced, priced and packaged. The pizzerias in Brooklyn all looked about the same, simple designs with basic tables and chairs, a pick up window and soda dispenser. It appeared on the surface to be a simple operation compared to a full scale restaurant and he was right to a point considering the industry as a whole has a ninety percent failure rate.

He was convinced it would be a viable business to run and guessed he had the cash to get started since thirty-five thousand sounded like all the money in the world to him. He reasoned he would start earning an income the first day of operation and if he was careful with his expenses could make a go of it. Without asking for advice or help he set out to open his store.

Without a business plan, Robert shot from the hip. His first task was to find a reasonably priced store front near his home in order to have an easy commute. The available ones with the heaviest foot traffic were more expensive than the stores off the beaten track. He found one location that had been a pizzeria with all the equipment and furniture in place. It went out of business a year earlier. All it needed was a top to bottom cleaning, a fresh coat of paint and a new sign. He was ready to make that his choice when the real estate agent, perhaps sensing Robert's naiveté and inexperience, guided him to another nearby storefront for half the rent. The agent convinced Robert that the money he saved each month would allow him to buy all new equipment and furnishings rather than settling for the shop worn and tired looking shop he was ready to take. He even recommended a place to buy what he needed. The agent said this was a better location because it was within a block of a high school and the foot traffic during most of the year would be high. Robert signed a one year's lease, left a sizeable deposit and set out to do what he thought must be done next, buy equipment, furniture and a sign.

In all fairness, I do not know the real estate agent's motivation or skill level. Giving him the benefit, he may have thought he was guiding Robert in the right direction. Keep in mind I heard this story solely from Robert's perspective.

Robert found a restaurant equipment company and ordered whatever the salesman said he needed. He selected a nearly new oven, refrigerator and various platters, dishware and glasses. He set delivery for the first day he took the store keys. He was confident he was well on his way.

When not working his regular job, Robert visited his competition and studied their menus, prices and wine and beer selections. He purchased a cookbook to learn how to make pie and assorted side dishes. He experimented at home to refined his recipes. He attempted his first pizza in his home oven and was satisfied it wasn't difficult and with practice he could improve the quality and taste.

Delivery date arrived and Robert was excited he had keys in hand. He thought a few days at most and everything would be in place and ready to go. The delivery truck arrived, the crew unloaded the equipment onto the sidewalk, got a signature and prepared to leave. Robert stopped them and asked what about getting everything inside. The driver said, the order specified sidewalk delivery. Robert called the company and learned inside delivery was an extra charge. He also learned that installation was additional and the gas and electric connections must be in place. This was all new information to Robert. He agreed to pay for the inside delivery but the driver quickly pointed out the oven would not fit through the single wide front or back door. A double wide door must be installed and that required a building permit and time. He needed plumbers for restrooms and kitchen sinks, electricians for the hook up of at least 300 amps, a 2-inch gas line to supply the HVAC and pizza oven with enough volume and pressure to operate at full capacity. Robert learned he had rented an empty clothing store that had none of what was required for a restaurant. The estimated cost of the additional work surpassed what was left of his thirty thousand dollar inheritance. He was stymied.

With no one to turn to for help, he returned the equipment for a charge and had it put on hold until he resolved these issues. He realized his first location would have been easier since everything was in place. He tried to renegotiate the lease. The landlord, who owned both properties, was sympathetic. He agreed to let Robert take the abandoned pizzeria with all the equipment. Relieved, Robert agreed. He cancelled the equipment order and paid a hefty restocking fee.

Robert began the remolding of his store with paint, some new furnishings, wall decorations and ordered a new sign for the front. When he tried to order food supplies from the wholesalers, they asked for a copy of his business license and resale certificate number. Robert had no idea what they were talking about nor how to get them. He learned he needed a tax id, a liquor license if he wanted to sell wine and beer, business insurance, Health Department and Building Department inspections. All this would take several months to get in place. He was paying rent on a store and no income other than his low paying job. Time was running out.

The final blow came when his application for a liquor license was denied because the pizzeria was within five hundred feet of a school. He was counting on the sale of wine and beer to increase his profit.

There were other things that were a surprise to him like needing a permit to change the store signage and getting incorporated. Unfortunately, he did not have the financial capital to tide him over. The end came after six months when he could no longer pay his rent or utility bills. He called the landlord and defaulted on the lease. He had no choice but to walk away. His inheritance was gone before he could sell his first pie.

The landlord got the benefit of Robert's rent money and hard work cleaning the place making it easier to rent to the next tenant. The restaurant equipment company made money on shipping and restocking equipment that was never unpacked. It was akin to putting inheritance in a pile and setting it on fire. All this could have been avoided if Robert had substantial experience in all aspects of the restaurant business and knew the process of opening a business. One quick call to the Small

Business Administration and he would have the resources of experienced business leaders who would guide him along the way.

Robert lamented, "If I had only known what I was getting into, I'd have just put the inheritance in the bank and saved it. How was I supposed to know all that stuff? I thought opening a little pizza pallor would be a synch. Now those people have my money and I have nothing. I'd do a better job if I took another shot at it but I have no money to get started. I blew my one chance."

I felt bad for John and didn't want to rub it in, but I think if he had another chance, he'd still fail. What did he know of bookkeeping, payroll taxes, hiring and firing, ordering the correct amount of supplies, budgeting for the slow season, negotiating with vendors, marketing and advertising? And he still had no experience baking pizzas on a large scale. Was he going to let his first customers be his Guiena pigs till he figured out what the heck he was doing? All things he never had to deal with because he gave up. He simply didn't know what he didn't know.

**A Case Study in Smart Money**

In one of my business classes, my professor relayed this success story on how things should be done.

A couple we will call Anthony and Marie, had a similar dream as Robert. Tired of working for others, they had dreamed of opening their own pizzeria. That is where the similarities ended.

Anthony had spent the last fifteen years or so working in the restaurant industry. He started out as a busing tables at a neighborhood restaurant, then he moved onto the kitchen washing dishes and keeping the kitchen area clean. He began waiting tables during the slow days to gain experience and then on to the busier nights. He changed jobs and started at a larger restaurant as a waiter and after two years he was promoted to head waiter. A year later he was front end manager where he was involved in managing the wait staff, hiring training and on occasion firing.

The owner liked Anthony's attitude and wanted him to have more responsibility. He took on added work of managing the back end of the restaurant which had doubled in size since he first started. Anthony helped the chef in prep work, ordering supplies and dealt with the health department to insure the restaurant always had an A plus rating.

The things Anthony was not familiar with were the negotiations with landlords, bill paying, payroll and advertising.

His wife, Marie, was a bookkeeper at a retail clothing chain and was responsible for payroll, receivables, sales tax payments negotiations with vendors and the landlords at a dozen locations. She had a decade of experience.

After setting aside seventy-five thousand dollars as startup money they began writing their business plan for their pizzeria. They met with the Division of Small Business which is part of New York State Development where they received mentoring for their pizzeria from seasoned professionals. They created a detailed check list of everything they needed to do before they opened their restaurant. Tony took Italian cooking classes and a job working in a pizzeria to learn how to make pizzas and some of the other dishes they offered. After a few months he felt confident to work on his own.

Anthony and Marie's experiences complemented each other and they were prepared for the problems and issues that cropped up. They had the resources to carry them over for the first six months, and after that their pizzeria was a success. After a few years they opened a second location and a third one is planned.

# Rule of 72
## and why the Smart Money starts saving early in life.

This is a guideline more than a hard and fast rule. The purpose is to help investors determine how long a particular investment will take to double their money. By dividing the interest rate into 72, the remainder will tell you how many years it takes your investment to double based on compound interest.

An example would be you are earning 10% on an investment of $1,000. By dividing 10 into 72, the remainder is 7.2. (72 / 10 = 7.2) Therefore, it will take 7 years 3 months for your original investment to double to $2,000.

Definition of terms:

APY shows you how much you'll earn in interest accrued over the course of a year. - http://twocents.lifehacker.com/ A savings account that has an APY of 1.005% would earn $10.05 in interest for the year for a total of $1010.05.

"A Money Market Account is a type of savings account that usually earns a higher amount of interest than a basic savings account. The minimum balance for this account is often considerably higher than the minimum balance of a basic savings account." - https://www.key.com

A Mutual Fund is an investment made up of a pool of funds collected from many investors for the purpose of investing in securities such as stocks. Think of it as everyone in your office chipping in to buy 1,000 lottery tickets. Your chances of winning are increased 1,000 times as opposed to you only buying one ticket. Your share of any prizes will be split but you have a better chance of winning something. The same is true of a Mutual Fund. One major fund has 212 different stocks in their portfolio. With a $1,000 initial investment, at a price of $12 a share, you could own 83 shares of the fund and benefit from the growth of all 212 companies. If one or two of those companies fall on hard times, the impact on the fund would be minimal.

**Examples:**

A certain bank's Money Market pays 1.26% APY. $1,000 invested at this rate would take 57 years to double your money. (72 / 1.26 = 57)

A bank's 5-year CD that pays 1.35% APY would take 53 years to double your money (72 / 1.26 = 53)

A bank's 5 year CD that pays 2% would need 36 years to double.

(72 / 2 = 36)

A Brokerage House's Mutual Fund that has a 15% return would need a little less than 5 years to double compared to the 1.26% APY bank CD which would take most of your life to double to $2,000.

Now invest $1,000 today in a Mutual Fund with a return of 15% without investing one more dollar and see what happens.

**Year - Value**

2016 - $1,000

2021 - $2,000

2026 - $4,000

2031 - $8,000

2037 - $16,000

2042 - $32,000

2047 - $64,000

2051 - $128,000

2056 - $256,000

2061 - $512,000

2066 - $1,024,000

In 50 years your account would double 10 times. A 20 year old who started today could look forward to over one million dollars by the time he or she is 70. A secure future from one investment of $1,000.

There are many things to consider.

The mutual fund can grow in price yielding a larger amount.

An initial investment of $2,000 would hit a million in less than 40 years.

You continue to invest each paycheck over your life time in a variety of funds for a balanced approach.

A million dollars would have less buying power in 50 years than today making it critical to make regular contributions to your portfolio. It doesn't have to be much and as little as $100 a month would be an extra $1,200 and year growing for you. (See the compound Interest Calculator below.)

You can never withdraw any money from this special account until you retire, otherwise you won't realize your goal.

If you wait until you're 50 to start saving for retirement, using the Rule of 72, you'd need to invest over $50,000 to achieve the same results by the time you are about 75.

With the bank CD, assuming the rates never change, it would take 1,000 years to reach one million dollars.

Mutual Funds fluctuate in price and some run out of steam while new opportunities come along. You need to monitor your investments. You can't put them on automatic pilot.

Don't put all your eggs in one basket, to quote a cliché. Diversify. Read the financial news online and see the top performing funds across many industries. Chose those you are familiar with first. As an example, if you are in computer technology, use your professional insight to find a fund that makes the most sense to you. Or, you may know enough that you decide to avoid any technology funds. That is as much a valid decision as buying into it.

Here is an unbiased tutorial on Mutual Funds

http://www.investopedia.com/video/play/introduction-mutual-funds/

An online calculator provided by the US Securities and Exchange Commission has an easy to use investment calculator.

https://www.investor.gov/additional-resources/free-financial-planning-tools/compound-interest-calculator

I used this to set up a savings program based on a $1,000 initial investment and $83 a month contribution which equals adding just $1,000 a year.

This is for a 20 year old who wants to build a savings account for the next 40 years. Regardless of your age, use this and determine how much you need to invest for retirement.

**A Case Study in Stupid Money**

A 63 year old single man we shall call Hank never was able to save for retirement. He always had an excuse, the first being the mistaken belief that Social Security was a pension. It's actually a safety net meant to supplement your retirement.

Although he lived within his means and rarely went into debt he saw no urgency to set aside anything for retirement. As a young man his explanations included, he couldn't afford to save anything, he needed every dime of his paycheck for living expenses and he had plenty of time to worry about it. He passed up on his companies generous 401k plan that matched contributions dollar for dollar as well as the ability to purchase company stock without paying a commission. Each year, during his performance review, his manager urged him to sign up for the programs. He laughed it off with "I'm gonna work until I drop dead."

At age 63 Hank found himself out of work due to downsizing during the recession. After two years of job searching, while living off of early Social Security, he was forced to take a minimum wage job at a big box store doing menial labor when his 99 weeks of Unemployment ran out.

Hank was shocked to learn his Social Security was less than two-thousand dollars a month. He somehow thought it would match his income from work. He admitted he never bothered to read the notices the Social Security Administration sent him each year outlining his benefits. To do so was tantamount to admitting he was getting old.

He now regrets his cavalier attitude about saving as he sees his friends and colleagues enjoying a great retirement. At 64. he manages to put money away from each paycheck but it will never be enough and one day he will be too old to work.

## A Case Study in Smart Money- MAYBE

Every Certified Financial Planner, every Stock Broker and every advisor will tell you never do what I did to build up a savings account. They will foam at the mouth, as they pound their first on the table, declaring it's not smart, it's stupid and a plan for disaster. And they are right for a large percentage of the public. What I did, was unthinkable. I borrowed money to buy stocks. Not a margin account, but a bank loan.

When I was in my middle twenties and engaged, I was talking to my Fiancés Uncle William. He was a soft spoken, kindly man who was a machinist for most of his life. His goal was to buy a house for his family in a decent neighborhood. He wasn't worried about retirement because he had a Union Pension to fall back on along with Social Security.

He told me when he was a young man in the 1940s, he went to a local bank and borrowed $300 ($4,000 in today's dollars*) for the purpose of opening his first savings account. He used the money as the collateral and each payday, he'd make a payment on the loan. Although long before my time, I've heard it was not an unusual practice. I asked why he didn't just open an account and make a deposit each payday. He said he tried doing it but something always came up and he never managed to save much. However, with that bill due each month, he made sure the payment went in on time. I don't know what the savings account paid in interest nor what the loan rate was back then, but Uncle William said it balanced out to just a few points in interest paid.

* http://www.usinflationcalculator.com/

After two years, Uncle William paid the loan in full. He had the $300 account that had earned interest for two years. He immediate borrowed another $500 and repeated the process. He continued this for a decade until he had enough saved for the down payment and an established credit history for his first house. He went one step further, the home he bought, in Woodhaven New York, was a two-family house. The tenants rent paid the mortgage and the property taxes. He and his wife lived there until they passed. Shortly before he died, Uncle William told me, "Counting the loans I repaid and the rental income from the tenants, we've owned this house for 25 years for free.

To me it sounded like a great idea. Four years after Uncle William told me this story, I was married with two children and living in a cramped apartment in Woodhaven. We had to move to a bigger home. There was no time to save for the down payment as Uncle William did. With some savings, along with a family loan, we were able to put the down payment on a Cape Cod on Long Island. We had used our last dollar moving in to the house save for a twenty dollar bill. In 1978, twenty dollars bought more than it did today. To put it in perspective, according to the inflation calculator, that $20 would be worth $73.82 in 2016 dollars. We had three days before my next paycheck and the money had to last. See: http://www.usinflationcalculator.com/

It was great that we had a home, but with no savings left, I began to panic. One missed mortgage payment and we could lose our house. About a month after we moved in, I received an offer from a local bank that congratulated us on our new home and with that letter, a check for $3,000. It was a loan, secured by our property and had an interest rate of about 10%. All I had to do is deposit it in the bank and I could use the money anyway I wanted.

The banks were paying less than 6% at the time if I followed Uncle Williams plan, it would be a net loss for me. I was also worried that as a home owner, I'd be tempted to waste the money on necessities. What I needed was an investment I'd be less likely to tap into. I had followed the stock market for years but never had the money to invest. I had an idea and this is the part where the Finical Advisors would freak out. I took the check to Fidelity Investments and approached the teller's window, I handed the clerk the check and asked if I could use it to open a brokerages account. He shrugged and replied, "There's only one way to find out and the worst thing they can do is say no."

I filled out the paperwork, deposited the check and asked for a relative safe investment. The clerk said they were not allowed to give recommendations on specific stocks but he could suggest I look at some Mutual Funds. He handed me a brochure and sort of indicated several funds that had a 10 % return rate. I read the perspective of each and decided on one fund and placed the order. In one month I had gone from nothing to owning a home and having a $3,000 stock portfolio.

My wife was a stay at home mom and the responsibility of earning an income fell on me. I knew I needed to make the monthly payments on the mortgage, utilities, home owners insurance and needed repairs, now I had to make a monthly payment on the bank loan. I quickly found two part time jobs that would not interfere with my full time sales position. I worked as a bartender on Friday and Saturday nights at a College pub and I delivered the Sunday New York Times every week. All in all, I earned an extra $90 a week ($332 in 2016 dollars) I repaid the loan ahead of schedule, which reduced the interest payments. The mutual fund grew at a faster pace than I expected. Within a year the loan was repaid and the fund was worth about $3,400, free and clear. As an example, if you borrow money for ten years at eight percent interest and you pay off the loan in five years, your net interest paid would be four percent.

A month after the loan was paid, I received another letter from the bank thanking me for being a great customer and for making timely payments. This time they included a loan check for $5,000. I discussed this with my wife and she was OK with it as long as the payments didn't cut into the household budget.

I had spent the last year reading the financial pages of the Sunday newspaper I was delivering and had acquired more knowledge on the various mutual funds, what was growing, which ones were staying flat.

This time I was a better informed investor and split the $5,000 between several funds.

By 1981, I was working for Procter & Gamble as a sales rep. It was a better paying job than I had before and had great benefits including a company car, health insurance and college tuition assistance. I signed up for all benefits including payroll deductions for savings bonds and company stock.

Because of the company car, I was able to sell one of our personal car and put the money towards paying off the bank loan. We saved about $900 a year on the costs of owning the car plus had health insurance now that P&G was providing it. I could return to college at night to get my bachelor's degree. The increase in pay plus the savings on car and health insurance allowed me to quit my part time jobs and spend more time with my family.

When the second bank loan was paid off, they sent me a check for $7,000 and I invested it as well. According to my records, my portfolio was about $25,000 not including my savings bonds and company stock. (About $60,000 in today's dollars.)

And that is how I started saving for my retirement. It was the last time I borrowed to purchase stocks. Yes I was fortunate to land a job at P&G and later Janssen Pharmaceutica, a division of Johnson & Johnson. I was fortunate to have family who could help us with the down payment on a house. I know not everyone has these opportunities and the business climate has drastically changed from the 1980s but the Rule of 72 still applies and the sooner you start saving the better off you will be when it counts.

Use the interest calculator and play around with the numbers to see what works for you at your age. Start saving and investing sooner rather than later. Start reading the financial pages online or in the papers. There are investment clubs everywhere you can join for free. There you will get sound advice from folks who aren't trying to sell you something.

## Pay yourself first.

As my best friend Peter, who passed away way too soon, told me, "When you get your paycheck, the first person you pay is yourself. Let your creditors fight over whatever is left."

How do you do that? The first thing you do is set aside a specific amount each paycheck and deposit into your savings or brokerage account. If your company has a 401k plan, use it to start your retirement account.

## Lease or Purchase a Car

There is no hard and fast rules for buying a car or truck for personal use regardless if it's new, used or leased. It depends on your personal situation and your goals.

Let's define the basics. Buying a new car has it's pluses and minuses. On the positive side, you can take advantage of zero or near zero percentage financing. Although, you should avoid debt whenever possible, it's Smart Money that takes advantage of free money, or what seems to be free money, to purchase a necessity.

What is Zero Percent financing? You will not see a bank offer zero financing on cars. These are loans offered by manufactures in an effort to sell a certain model or slow moving vehicles a dealership has in inventory. This is often offered at the end of a season to help clear the lots to make room for the next years models. A dealership may offer zero financing by assuming the interest charged by a lender.

To qualify for the loan, to coin a phrase, you don't need the money. They are reserved for Tier 1 credit scores, usually above 700. This can vary from manufacturer and region of the country. Even if your credit score is slightly below the threshold, you may still qualify if you have a solid payment history or are brand loyal.

The option to zero finance is cash back where you get a rebate check for paying cash. Here is a great calculator to help determine what is best for you: http://www.edmunds.com/calculators/incentives-rebates.html

In short, there is a break-even point. According to the Edmunds calculator, on a $32,600 loan that includes tax and fees vs a $2,500 cash back for paying cash, you should take the cash back option.

Low APR

Total Loan Amount: $32,600

Monthly Payment (Using Special Dealer Rate) $543

Cash Back

Total Loan Amount: $30,100

Monthly Payment (Using Customer Cash Rebate) $541

In this case, it's a toss up.

Taking the cash will save you $3 per month or $180 over a 60 month loan. It is a break-even point, but the calculator will give you the best option.

If you think $3 a month is chump change, then I challenge you to walk into any car dealership an drop $180 ($3 a month x 60 months) on the desk and walk out with nothing to show for it, Go ahead, I dare you.

Guarantees and Warranties are words often interchanged.

As the saying goes, "A guarantee is only as good as the person who gave it." Unlike the past, today's new cars come with three year or 50,000 mile warrantees. Some come with 10 year or 100,000 mile limited warrantees. The key word here is limited.

A full warrantee is an offer to repair or replace the item if defective within a certain amount of time. A limited warrantee may only cover certain parts but not the labor to replace them. Both can be voided if the car is misused or you have unauthorized repairs performed.

Beware the fine print

Take time to read the fine print in newspaper or online ads. Often the restrictions are buried there. Here are some examples of "Gotch Ya's"

Must present ad at time of signing. (Left the Ad at home? – Too bad for you.)

Prior deals excluded. (Last week's special no longer applies.)

Must take same day delivery. (The next day doesn't qualify.)

All rebates are taxable in New York State. Other states may have other requirements. ($2,500 rebate times 8% tax equals an extra $200)

Minimum credit scores for special offers. (800 in some cases.)

Special discounts for loyal customers.(If you're a new customer, you pay more although exceptions are made depending how badly the dealership needs the sale.)

Special; discounts for recent graduates (What recent graduate has the cash or credit score to qualify?)

In 1984, I graduated from college after spending 10 years in night school. I was 35 years old and we needed a new car. The Pontiac salesman was surprised when I presented a copy of my diploma and transcript to prove I had graduated the prior week. He deducted $500 for the final price. He said it was the first recent grad car discount he had given in two years. It was an offer to attract attention but one that would seldom be used by customers. How many 22 year old grads can afford to buy a new car.

**Other pros of buying a new car.**

Aside from the obvious pride of ownership in a car no one else has driven and the new car smell, you get the latest technology and features. Often expensive options in the past are now included as standard equipment. For those of you too young to remember the 1960s, electric windows, cruise control, power seats, brakes and steering, high end stereo, and intermittent wipers were expensive add-ons for the top of the line cars. They are now available on economy cars along with GPS and back up cameras.

New cars come with a warranty covering anywhere from three years or 60,000 miles to 10-years, or 100,000 mile powertrain warranty that includes the engine and transmission. The dealer may even offer an extended warranty beyond the manufacturer's expiration date. But it is imperative that you read the fine print. You need to make sure it's backed by the automaker, not just the dealership or some other company. A manufacturer's-backed extended warranty can be used at any dealership across the country. A third-party warranty might be good only at the dealership that sold it to you which is of no help when your car breaks down 500 miles from home.

Manufacturers may offer you a choice of taking zero or low financing instead of a rebate. If you don't want to use your cash, use the rebate for the down payment. You can save hundreds to thousands of dollars in interest costs over the course of the loan but you need to study the numbers. Don't fall for high pressure sales tactics to get you to sign today. Both the dealership, the car and the deals will be there the next day.

**The Cons of buying a new car.**

Depreciation is the biggest downside of buying a new car. You can count on anywhere from 10 to 15 percent loss on your new car before you drive it of the lot. That means a $30,000 car will lose $3,000 to $3,500.

Edmunds has examples of new car depreciation.

http://www.edmunds.com/car-buying/how-fast-does-my-new-car-lose-value-infographic.html

Remember the more expensive the car the higher the depreciation.

Consider you pay cash for a $32,000 car. As soon as you take ownership, before you even sit behind the wheel, it has depreciated at least $3,500 or 25%. A year later, assuming it is well maintained, the vale has depreciated about $8,000 or 25%. In three years it's worth about half of what you paid.

Yes, desirable cars and trucks depreciate slower than less popular ones and convertibles hold their value better. But they do fall in value quicker than if you bought a one year old car off the dealer's used car lot.

If you decide to buy a new one, plan on holding it for ten years. By that time the year to year depreciation will be insignificant.

Remember

When the top goes down, the price goes up.

4 doors is 2 doors 2 many.

**The Pros and Cons of buying a used car.**

There are three choices for used cars:

Buying a used luxury car from a dealer.

Buying a used economy or standard car from a dealer.

Buying any used car privately or through an auction.

I prefer buying a used cars and only from a manufacturer's dealer. In other words, a used Chevy from a Chevrolet or other GM dealership. I would never buy a used Volvo or other high end car from a Chevy dealer. If I want a Volvo, I'll get it from a Volvo dealership and nowhere else. If I want a Jeep, I'll get it from a Chrysler dealership*.

Who better knows the car that the manufacturer's trained mechanics? I have to ask if the Volvo on the Chevy's lot is so good, why isn't it on the Volvo's lot. There can be several reasons for this. One is the original Volvo owner traded his or her car in for a Chevy for any variety of reasons including they couldn't afford another high end car or they inherited the car and didn't care for it. Another is the dealer bought the

Volvo from an auction. The first reason is a reasonable scenario and the car may be perfectly fine, but the Chevy technicians aren't trained on the evaluation or servicing other manufacturer's cars.

If the Chevy dealer bought the Volvo at auction, why didn't a Volvo dealer buy the car instead? Either they didn't see it, bid on it but the selling price got too high, or saw it and didn't want it because they have intimate knowledge. Perhaps it was a model or year that had to many issues and the Volvo dealership steered clear of it. You will never know. Why take the chance?

This is no reflection on the competency of a Chevy mechanic. They are well trained by the manufacturer, but it's not their area of expertise. You can have the same issues with a Cadillac on a Mercedes Benz dealership's used car lot. This is even more relevant with today's car computers. Manufacturers don't like to share their technical specifications with mechanics outside their network. About ten years ago I owned a Saab. (now out of business) and finding someone to service it was impossible because Saab didn't share their technical information and parts were hard to come by. In the end, I traded the car for a lot less than it was worth.

A friend bought a used high end foreign car form a domestic car used lot. The car developed a problem shortly after he picked it up. He returned it to the dealer who had to send it out to the foreign car dealership to get it fixed. They did, but only after a three week wait. The foreign car dealership may have put this car at the bottom of their priority list because they wanted to help their own customers first.

I purchased a used Volvo from a Volvo dealership and had a similar issue. I took it back to the dealer and they fixed it immediately because I was their customer, it was their brand of car, they had the trained techs, replacement parts on hand and equipment to fix it.

**The Pros of buying a used car**

The biggest advantage is you can get a higher quality car with more options for the same price of a lower-end new model. Assume you wanted to spend $30,000 on a new luxury hardtop sedan. Well the dealer happens to have, for $3,500 less, a two-year-old convertible with just under 8,000 miles on it? If you're a diehard convertible freak like me, it's a no brainer, a tempting proposition. But is it a good choice?

The possibilities are endless. Depending on the make, model, year, condition and mileage you can have many choices. This is why you have to do your homework, narrow down your picks and be prepared to shop around. The internet has made this easier. Smart Money will log onto a free service like https://www.truecar.com/ and enter what they want in a car and the service will send the request to different dealerships in an area. The dealers bid on the business. Stupid money does no homework, walks onto a lot and lets the salesman guide their choices. It's so much easier to let someone else make the decisions for you. All Stupid Money does is sign papers and write a check.

But you need to do the research first, know what you want and avoid the initial depreciation.

Only buy a Certified Pre Owned used car. (CPO)

A CPO is a late model used car offered through dealerships. They are guaranteed to be fully inspected, refurbished and often include an extended warranty. There may be other benefits included along with special financing and scheduled maintenance. Keep in mind each manufacturer and dealership will offer different packages.

Find out of the CPO is from the dealership or from the manufacturer which is preferable. If the CPO is from the manufacturer then you can go to any dealership for repairs. If it is from the dealership you have to return to the place where you bought the car. For a low priced, older used car a CPO is rarely an option.

For more information on CPOs read the article on cars.com or you can Google Pros and Cons of certified preowned used cars.

http://www.cars.com/go/advice/shopping/cpo/stories/story.jsp?story=prosCons

You may consider buying another brand car from a dealer's used car lot at the end of the month when the sales reps are pressured to hit quota. The Chevy dealer will view the odd looking Nissan Cube on his lot as a UFO and just wants to be rid of it. You can actually pick up a bargain doing this but you have to know your stuff.

**The Cons of buying a used car**

The running joke is a used car salesman who told the sucker the car was driven by a little old lady who only drove it to church on Sundays. The customer believed the story, bought the car only to learn the car was completely worn out. My parent's generation said they would not buy a used car because they didn't want to pay for the last owners troubles. They walked past the dealer's used car lot and plopped down their money for a brand new car. A Depression mentality had a role in it as well. They had lived so long with left overs and worn out jalopies that couldn't wait for a new car.

The reality is you do not know who drove the car before you, how they drove, how well they maintained it or why they sold it. You can't just take the sales person's word for it. Many from my parent's generation walked past the dealer's used car lot and plopped down their money for a brand new car.

Today, we have services like CarFax that removes the guesswork. They supply you with the following:

Title information, including salvaged or junked titles

Flood damage history

Total loss accident history

Odometer readings

Lemon history

Number of owners

Accident indicators, such as airbag deployments

State emissions inspection results

Service records

Vehicle use (taxi, rental, lease, etc.)

The last three cars I purchased came with the CarFax report. It was supplied by the dealer. I didn't have to ask for it. If the dealer does not offer it, go to the CarFax website and follow the instructions. There is a fee but it can save you from buying a headache.

I would never buy a used car from a private seller or a small car lot. You are taking a chance even with a CarFax report. You are usually getting nothing more than a 30 day limited warranty from the car lot and no warranty from the private seller. You have no idea what has been done to the car by the individual or used car dealer.

Thirty years ago, I had friends who were good mechanics and could spot a bargain. They would buy off of a lot, an auction or from a private seller, knowing what to look for, fix it themselves and either resell it for a profit or keep the car. We called them shade tree mechanics.

Today's cars are far more sophisticated and most have proprietary software that only the dealers can service. Some new cars have eliminated the oil and transmission dipsticks. If you want to check the fluid levels before making a trip you have to take it to the dealer and have them do it. I was outraged that this information was help from me on my last purchase. I was incensed that he withheld the information. I would have bought the car anyway but I would have been aware. Even if they didn't charge me for checking, the dealership is a 20 minute drive each way. A friend had bought a new car a few years ago and it began running rough. He was an old-school shade tree mechanic like me and took matters on his own. He removed the four spark plugs, cleaned and replaced them. When the car would not start, he called the dealership and learned the car must be hooked up to a computer before the plugs can be replaced. He had to have the car towed to the dealer and paid to fix it. About all you can check is tire pressure, windshield washer, brake and power steering fluid. Everything is managed by the dealer.

YouTube is a great resource to try if you want to attempt a minor repair on your own. Do your research before you buy any car, especially a used one from a private seller as well as a used car lot.

A website http://www.testingautos.com/ will give you a breakdown of any car or model you are interested in. As an example they report the maintenance cost on a high end German car will cost about $15,000 over a 5 year period and a comparably sized and equipped Japanese car will cost about $5,000 in maintenance for the same period of time.

Smart money does their homework. Stupid money buys on impulse.

**Leasing a car**

The similarity between renting a car and leasing one is you are paying for the right to use a car owned by someone else. The difference is the rental agreement is for a short period of time from a day to a week with unlimited mileage and your choices are from an inventory on hand by the rental company. There is no option to buy the car at the end of the rental period.

When you lease a car, it is generally for three years with limited mileage with the option to buy the car at the end of the lease. The cost for a rental is on average about $30 a day while the leased car would run about $12 a day.

The other difference is the rental company only requires that you have a credit card while a leasing company will run a credit check on you and require that you have auto insurance.

While leasing is smart for some people, it's stupid for others. Unlike the clearly defined smart and stupid money when it comes to savings, the lines are blurred with leasing a car.

An independent insurance broker may find it's best to lease a mid-size sedan for entertaining clients while the owner of a construction company will buy a pick up because of the extensive wear and tear the truck will endure on the job site. Both can take a business deduction but in different ways. Their accountants can determine what is best.

An individual may like the flexibility of leasing since they can upgrade to a better car than they could afford buying new and have the ability to drive a new car every three years. If done the right way it makes sense. The difference between Smart Money and Stupid Money is understanding the pitfalls.

A dealer will advertise low monthly lease rates to draw customers into the show room without being upfront about the true costs. For example, in my local newspaper, Newsday, a dealer advertises an All-Wheel Drive (AWD) crossover with options for $169 a month for 36 months.

Stupid Money will rush down and lease the car thinking they can drive a new car for very little money. Smart Money will read the fine print and understand there is an $1,800 down payment and a $600 bank fee bringing the actual cost to $236 a month. The $1,800 down payment, sometimes called a cap reduction fee, is just an upfront lease payment as is the bank fee. Smart Money see that the lease is limited to 10,000 driven miles per year or 833 miles per month. Smart Money knows he or she drives on average of 20,000 miles a year. The overage charge is 18 cents a mile. The difference between allowed mileage and actual miles driven amounts to a $5,400 surcharge at the end of the lease. Instead of the low teaser rate of $169, Smart Money sees the actual cost of the lease is $386 a month, more than twice the advertised price. If you know you drive more than the allotted amount you can negotiate better rate than 18 cents per mile. Stupid Money has no clue of any of this. All they see is $169 for a new Crossover.

What Stupid Money learns is that due to his low credit score, the lease payment is substantially higher. Meanwhile Smart Money finds a similar Crossover at a competing dealer with upfront pricing and more allowed mileage.

Some of the things to consider when leasing a car:

When you prepay the lease as in the $1,800 down payment and the car is stolen or destroyed in an accident, the Insurance company will cover the value of the car but you can say goodbye to the down payment. You most likely will never have that money refunded to you. Smart Money will find a lease with nothing down even if the monthly payment is higher. In the above case $1,800 divided by 36 months equals $50 a month.

Smart Money sees a $219 monthly lease with no down payment equal to a $169 lease with an $1,800 down payment.

That $1,800 is protected in case the car is totaled or stolen.

Stupid Money can't get past the $169 teaser price.

Smart Money buys Gap Insurance

The value of any car, new used or leased, drops significantly after it's driven off the lot. If the leased car is stolen or totaled, the Insurance company will pay the value of the car. If that doesn't cover the total obligation you have with the lease agreement, you will have to pay the difference unless you have Gap Insurance (Guaranteed Auto Protection) that cover the difference or the GAP. You don't want to pay an additional $5,000 on a car you no longer own. This may or may not be included with the lease. You have to ask. If it's not then you should find a better deal.

**End of lease wear and tear**

When you return the car at the end of the lease, you will be held responsible for any damage beyond normal wear and tear along with mileage beyond the agreed amount. Each manufacturer, each dealer and each inspector has their own standards of wear and tear. Don't be shocked if you're handed a bill for $300 for a new tire with excessive wear on it. By the time you get the bill the car will be gone and you can't inspect it. I turned in a leased Saab and was later told there was paint damage along the passenger side and a badly worn tire. Fortunately, I had taken a video of the car's interior and exterior as well as the tires. The dealer backed off.

Ask about the terms and conditions when you first lease the car. Know what the guidelines are before you sign. Some dealers say if the damage is smaller than the size of a credit card it is considered normal wear and tear. Others may say it has to be smaller than a quarter. Minor chips and scratches are allowable but some may nitpick the car to death to get more money out of you, offer to waive the charges if you lease a new car or to convince you to buy the car outright.

If you return the car with excessive damage expect to pay full retail price for the repairs. If the car is in an accident, insist that the car is repaired at a shop the dealership uses. If the repairs are not up to the dealer's standards, you may be liable for the work to be corrected. For the most part, insurance companies will not have the car repaired through a dealership because of the dealer's mark up for handling the repairs. But you have the right to get the car repaired correctly.

The dealer may waive the damages or excessive mileage if you agree to lease a new car. They may also offer you a deal to purchase the car thus avoiding any fees. Those options are up to you and there is no right or wrong answer. You have intimate knowledge of the car after driving it for 36 months. Consider the maintenance costs of luxury cars vs standard ones. YourMechanic.com has a list of the maintenance costs of most cars. It can be found at:

https://www.yourmechanic.com/article/the-most-and-least-expensive-cars-to-maintain-by-maddy-martin

**Buying at Auction**

Smart money avoids auctions unless they are car dealers or trained mechanics and know what to look for. Stupid money can't get past the cheap price and buys one.

What I learned from an auctioneer was the pros know what cars to buy, what to pay and what to avoid. All of the bargains are snapped up. What is left over is the junk that Stupid Money buys.

CarsDirect.com has a great article on the pros and cons of auction buying.

http://www.carsdirect.com/used-car-buying/pros--cons-of-used-car-auctions

**What is an AS IS car**

It is a car with no warrantee or guarantee. You buy it, you own it. If the engine blows the moment you drive it off the lot, you're stuck with the repairs. The used car you buy from a neighbor is sold As Is. Let the buyer beware.

## A case study in Stupid Money

A used car lot advertised, "Any truck on our lot is priced to sell. Bad Credit - No Credit - No problem. Fully guaranteed for one year."

All that you needed was $1,400 down payment. Some dishonest locals scrapped up the $1,400 and bought one of the trucks listed for $5,000 with no intention of making any future payments. The truck only ran for a several months and when it broke down, the owner towed in it for the repairs only to learn that since they had never made a payment, the guarantee was null and void. If by chance the customer made the payments, the used car lot made good on its pledge and fixed no matter what was wrong with the truck. The bottom line was the trucks were only worth $1,400.

# Poverty is a State of Mind

It has nothing to do with a lack of money.

Consider the woman who won $10,000,000 after taxes in the lottery. Nine years later she is living paycheck to paycheck from her part time job to support her children. She had mismanaged the money.

A couple never seemed to have enough food on hand to feed their children even though they both worked and lived modestly. They had a fixed budget for food, kept track of how much they were spending and when they reached the limit stopped shopping even though they had not bought the staple items they needed.

The husband worked for a small transmission repair shop and complained to his boss that he needed a raise to buy enough food for his family. The owner felt the mechanic had earned enough to provide food especially since the wife worked as well. The owner agreed to consider it but only if his wife could accompany the couple grocery shopping, They agreed.

At the store, the couple took a shopping cart and began on the far left hand aisle. They picked up a case of beer and entered the price on to their calculator, Then they moved to the soft drink aisle and loaded the cart with 6 liter bottles of soda. They did the same as they went through the snack aisle and bought chips, cookies and brownie mix. They made it as far as the frozen food section, bought two gallons of premium ice cream, entered the amount on the calculator and proclaimed, "You see? We're out of money and still haven't bought any milk, eggs, bread or cereal. How can we live on what your husband pays me?"

The owner's wife patiently explained they should start shopping on the right hand side of the store, buying the staple items first, looking for sales, store brands and using coupons. If there was any money left, they could afford some treats for the family.

The couple were startled at the results. After more coaching the couple learned how to better manage their budget. They had plenty of food and often had money left over. They learned to wait for double coupon days to stretch their budget further. It was that no one had ever shown them how to shop. They went from making stupid money decisions to smart ones overnight.

A single mom is desperate to find work. She walks through her small town's business district and knocks on each door begging for a job. Her persistence paid off when she was offered good paying employment at a print shop but when she is told she has to climb a flight of stairs to the office, she turned the job down. She claimed she was fit and able to climb stairs but it was just too inconvenient. She moved on to the next business and tried again.

A wealthy couple lost everything when the six figure incomes both had dried up. They thought the gravy train would never end and saw no need to save for the proverbial rainy day. When that day came, they had to walk away from their home, lavish furnishings and luxury cars. Both settled for low pay jobs and to this day never recovered their former lifestyle.

I refuse to call anyone of these people stupid but I will say they exhibited poor money management skills that had a devastating effect on their lives.

It isn't the lack of education either. The wealthy couple who lost it all were both college educated and stepped into high paying jobs straight out of college. Money came easily to them. Their lack of foresight was their down fall. They both exhibited a high degree of intelligence in which to do their jobs but when it came to managing their personal money, they spent it as fast as it came in. They joined an expensive country club that they rarely attended because of their busy schedules. A surprising decision since neither one played golf.

They leased two high end SUVs even though they drove to work together in the husband's car. At the end of the lease, they turned in the wife's rarely used SUV with less than 8,000 miles on the odometer. They were allowed 36,000 miles. They leased her a new SUV the same day. When his SUV was at the end of its lease, it had more than 12,000 miles of excessive mileage which cost them 25 cents per mile, a $3,000 penalty. What prevented them from alternating the cars when one was close to the mileage limit?

They bought an expensive time share at a prime resort because it was what their friends were doing, but after six years they had used it once. Each year they had a new destination for a vacation and decided to forgo the time share and simply pay the maintenance fees.

You can't call them irresponsible. Their jobs carried the weight for an entire department with complicated research and development budgets in an ever evolving technical industry. They had to account for every dollar and ensure is was well spent.

If they had millions of dollars in savings that drew enough interest and dividends to pay for their life style, it would have been sustainable. But they didn't have any money saved and their house was heavily mortgaged. With $250,000 a year in combined income after taxes they lived on all of it. When the dot com bubble burst, their company shut down and overnight they were unemployed and except for some jewelry furnishings and wardrobes, they had no assets. They had little to show after a decade of a high income. The one thing they did that was smart was to avoid credit debt.

A child born into poverty where both parents worked had a different approach to money management as he grew up. His parents didn't squander whatever money they earned, they just didn't earn a lot. They impressed upon him the need to get an education and pursue the American dream they had been unable to achieve. When he made his first fortune selling his software company, he provided for his parents.

Rich or poor, educated or not, poverty is a state of mind that dictates how one manages money. While some languish in low pay jobs they live simple lives and save for the future.

A young man earns $10 an hour at a big box store. He lives alone in a studio apartment in Queens for $500 a month. His monthly income less taxes is about $2,000 less the $500 in rent leaving $1,500 for basic needs. He works part time jobs on the weekend and manages to put $400 a month into his savings account. Even though it earns little interest, he socks away $4,800 a year. If nothing changes, in a decade he will have saved $50,000.

Life happens. If he marries it will change his lifestyle. If he pursues a vocation or college he can find a better job and his income will rise. The point is he has the ability to grow his net worth in spite of being in a dead end job.

# Never Let Anyone Manage Your Money

Do your homework and make your own decisions.

1960 was a tough time to be a widowed mother of four living in Greenville South Carolina. It was my mother's fate after my father passed. While my older sister was married and in New York, there were three brothers aged four, nine (me) and fourteen that had to be raised and educated.

Job opportunities for women were limited to secretarial, working in a shirt factory, teaching and as a waitress. Since my mother had only a high school education, teaching was out. She needed an income to sustain the family. She told me that there had to be a better way than minimum wage jobs. She knew that wealthy people made their money in real estate and in the stock market. She and my father had built and flipped a few houses when he was alive but he was working at a good job and his income provided all we needed. In those days a family only needed one bread winner and the wife was the stay at home mom.

My mother dragged me to the library every Saturday morning to check-out books on real estate and the stock market. She must have plowed through a dozen books on each subject. She read the financial pages of the local paper each Sunday and the Wall Street Journal when we visited the library.

While she was able to flip a few houses each year, she saw the greatest opportunities on Wall Street. The problem in the 1960s was women didn't invest. It was a man's world. Although she could open an account with a brokerage, she had to use a broker who wanted to put her account into what was known as Widows and Orphans stocks. Those were investments that generated small dividends and considered safe havens. Mostly they were banks and utility stocks. Mutual Funds were around but limited in scope and numbers.

By 1961, my mother had gained enough knowledge of the market that she wanted to invest in her own stocks picks. She did her research and decided she wanted to buy a thousand shares of a company that had impressive sales. Her stock broker laughed at her. He said it was a flash in the pan and no business would buy a machine that made photocopies when carbon paper was ten cents a box. He would not place a trade for her to buy a thousand shares of Xerox. He flatly refused. My mother saw no way around him and missed an opportunity to get in on the meteoric rise of Xerox and would have made her a millionaire. And this was back when a million dollars was considered serious money.

From this experience, she taught me at a young age, never let anyone manage your money. Do your homework, make your own decisions and stick to your guns. She went on to find other tiny companies with great futures like Family Dollar Store and Danaher but that experience with Xerox turned her off from working with stock brokers. Eventually she opened an account with a discount brokerage, Fidelity.

One other experience happened when she wanted to buy into the an Initial Public Offering (IPO). Not having a computer background, she asked some friends about the company. They all "poo pooed" the idea and said there was no market for personal computers. She listened to them and did not buy Microsoft. Like her experience with Xerox, she didn't listen to her gut instinct.

When she had stumbled across a discount retailer named Family Dollar Store, she called the company and asked to speak to the CEO.

Surprisingly, he took the call. He spent an hour on the phone with my mother talking about their expansion, success and future plans. She bought thousands of shares at 19 cents a share. The stock split three times, paid a great dividend but when she could no longer manage her affairs and entered a nursing home, the financial planner dumped her shares. The stock has since risen to $80 a share.

# More Case Studies of Stupid Money
## The $6 Latte

The cost for a coffee shop to make a latte is about 86 cents. Add in labor and overhead and the stores cost is about a dollar.

Charisse was a receptionist at a small company. Her salary was based on her experience and performance. She was a diligent worker and never took time off. She complained to her manager that she didn't earn enough money to last her through the week. She said, "My life is pretty simple. I don't go out much, eat at home and only buy clothing on sale. I don't smoke and only drink if I'm at a party. I have basic cable service since I don't watch TV and don't splurge on fancy foods when I grocery shop. I don't know where the money goes."

Charisse arrived each morning on time with her double mocha latte and breakfast sandwich. Each week she had her hair done, a pedi, mani and ordered in lunch. She was a voracious reader and each week had the latest hard cover novel under her arm. Most of her business clothes were dry clean only even though the dress code was casual but neat.

The office manager offered some advice, "Charisse you spend about six dollars a day on the latte, sometimes having another one in the afternoon. You buy your breakfast sandwich at a deli and order in your lunch even though you say you don't eat out much. The pedi and manis cost you about $25 a week and your hair is another thirty dollars a week. As I see it you spend one hundred and fifty dollars a week on things you could do without. We have free coffee in the break room, someone always brings in some pastries or salad, or you could make your lunch at home and bring it in. I didn't include the money you spend on books but a new hard cover can run twenty-five dollars. Go to the library across the street from the office where you can check out books for free. You can even borrow CDs and movies. Do your own hair and nails and start buying wash and wear clothes and save another thirty dollars a week on dry cleaning. You can easily save ten thousand dollars a year and I promise you won't miss any of the things you are wasting money on now."

The young lady adjusted her spending habits over time and improved her situation.

## The 401k and a vacation home

Two New Yorkers, Frank and Maryann were in their mid-forties and both worked full time. She was a professional business woman and he was a Union electrician. Both had contributed to their retirement plan and were mostly debt free.

Frank responded to an online ad for a Condo in Central Florida. The price was $175,000 and he had more than enough in his 401k to cover the cost. Without consulting with his accountant or anyone who owned an out of state vacation home, they bought the condo sight unseen. They were impressed with the photos on line and the description. To pay for the condo, Frank took an early withdrawal from his 401k to avoid have a monthly mortgage payment and a huge debt.

In February the next year, they sent their documents to their accountant who prepared their tax returns. The accountant called Frank and asked, "What did you do? Do you have any idea what you have done to your retirement account? Do you know how much you owe the IRS and New York State? You only spend two weeks a year down there. For what you are spending, you two could fly to Europe every year and stay in a five star hotel. Why didn't you ask me first?"

Frank was shocked to learn they were responsible for income tax on the withdrawal and a 10% early withdrawal penalty. He had no idea the brokerage house withheld 20% of the withdrawal as required by law Their tax bill jumped by $100,000. They didn't have the savings to cover it and had to take a second mortgage to pay the tax bills. Instead of having a mortgage on a second home, they had a debt on their primary residence. If they defaulted they could lose their home. It was another landmine they could have avoided if they had asked their accountant before doing anything.

They were also stuck with the maintenance, taxes and insurance on a condo 1,500 miles away that was not near a hub airport making the air fare more expensive than other locations. In addition, they had to rent a car each time they visited, buy food plus all the household things like dishes, cooking utensils, utility bills, linen and other things you need to run a home, things Frank and Maryann never considered.

Most of the Condos went unsold in the building making it hard for the building to maintain the property. Over time the building started showing wear and tear depreciating the value. The cost of repairing a storm damaged roof was shared among the Condo owners costing Frank and . Maryann thousands more. To make things worse, they saw ads posted for resale Condos in the same neighborhood for half of what they paid.

Now they are stuck with a condo, monthly bills, a $100,000 debt and a retirement package literally cut in half all because of a spur of the moment purchase.

# Timeshare

A fancy word for putting your hard earned money in a pile
and setting it on fire.

My wife was always drawn in by the free gifts offered in exchange for a 60 minute presentation. I was dead set against timeshares because I knew they were the absolute worst investment to make. Yet many of our friends bought them and couldn't rave enough, until a few years later and the location became a bore with the monthly payments of over $500 a month at 11% interest plus maintenance fees began to pile up. As their families grew, the cost of travel became prohibitive. Attempts to swap out their slot for another location resulted in a summer time week in ski country or winter weeks at the beach.

After the fourth grueling presentation to get a free no-name toaster oven or tickets to a comedy show that reveled the audience in nonstop profanity, I declared I'd never attend another high pressure timeshare presentation. Without me tagging along, the resort wouldn't allow my wife to attend alone.

As a professional sales rep, armed with Fortune 50 company sales training and experience, I was immune to the high-pressure tactics. Often times I wanted to interrupt the presenter and give him/her advice on giving a presentation like not clasping their hands in front of their groin while speaking. It's a sign of insecurity and defensiveness. I wanted to walk up to the presenter and place my hands on his shoulders to stop him from rocking back and forth as he spoke. It makes the audience sea sick. Others let their voice trail off as they made their sales point or held the microphone too far away from their mouth rendering the mic useless.

One kept jabbing his finger at the audience. He looked aggressive, unwelcoming and off-putting to many in the crowd. But I restrained myself and let them blunder along. It wasn't my place and why would I help them fleece more people?

Google "timeshare nightmares" to get the first-hand accounts of those who caved in and purchased. One story is of a Honeymoon couple who were wined and dined until intoxicated only to wake the next morning to find they had signed on the dotted line for a thirty year commitment on a resort they really didn't like. When they complained, they were told "tough luck, you signed on the dotted line." Only after retaining an attorney did they learn there the state law provided them a ten day cooling off period. They managed to get a full refund but still had legal fees to pay. Learn the cooling off period for each state at this website: http://rcivip.com/timeshare-rescission-period-in-us/ in case you find yourself with buyer's remorse.

Gather the information online of these first person accounts, run the actual numbers of the cost and fees and see what the annual amount would be. Then check out an online service like Travelocity.com "Last Minute Deals" for hotels and airfare and see if you can't plan a better vacation for less money and for a different location that fits your timetable.

Quickenloans.com gas a great article on the pros and cons of timeshare.

https://www.quickenloans.com/blog/are-timeshares-worth-the-money

If we take the midrange of $10,000 cost plus $500 a month for maintenance, you will lay out $16,000 your first year and $6,000 a year moving forward. This does not include other fees that are tacked on or on transportation. Keep in mind you are tied into one location forever.

At Travelocity.com's "Last minute deals" I found a one week stay at a four start hotel with airfare for two adults for $1,000 per person including flight, hotel and fees. Toss in two kids aged 3 and 6 and another 4 star hotel is only $650 per person.

## Waiting for Politicians to Fix Your Problems

Nothing drives me battier than hearing someone say they will vote along a political party line because they feel their pain, work hard to help solve their problems and are champions of the little guy.

I ask, "You've been voting for them for 25 years and they haven't helped you one iota.

They say, "I need a better paying job and they promise to raise the minimum wage."

I say, "Get better skills so you can get a better paying job."

They say, "There are no better paying jobs. I know because I asked around."

I say, "You didn't ask around long enough. You gave up too soon."

They say, "What am I supposed to do?"

I say, "If you fell into a swimming pool would you try and swim to the edge and pull yourself out or slowly sink to the bottom waiting for the government to rescue you?

They say, "I would try and save myself because I can't swim very well and would surly drown."

I say, "If you get hungry do you make yourself lunch or wait for a politician to hand you a slice of pizza?"

They say, "I make myself lunch."

I say, "Then stop waiting for some self-serving politicians that really doesn't care if you live or die, prosper or struggle to make your life better. Go online and find careers that are hiring. Find out what skills you need and enroll at the local community college or trade school and get those skills."

They say, "But there are no great job where I live."

I say, "Then move to where the jobs are like I did when I graduated from High School."

They say, "But it could take me ten years to get my college degree."

I say, "How old will you be in ten tears if you don't get your degree?"

They say, "Well what happens in the meantime."

I say, "If a prospective employer sees you're attending college classes at night trying to improve yourself, it can open doors for you. It worked for me. As I earned more credits toward my degree in business, I was able to get promotions and better jobs."

Or you can wait for some back slapping, baby kissing, flip flopping politician to wave a magic wand and make your life better. The choice is yours.

# In Conclusion

No one cares more about your financial health and future more than you do. Think of managing your money as a part time job that will reap benefits for your entire life.

The internet if filled with websites that offer advice and remedies for almost every situation you could face. It is up to you to find them. Study them and heed their guidance. It will mean the difference between a comfortable retirement and one in which you struggle.

# ABOUT THE AUTHOR

Mike Swedenberg has been self-publishing books for over five years. He provides copywriting, coaching and teaches continuing education classes at Nassau Community College.

His educational background in business, sales, creative writing and marketing has given him a broad base from which to approach many topics.

His writing skills is confirmed independently on Amazon.com He especially enjoys producing study guides and self-help books.


Sam Chinkes

Las Vegas, NV.


**Other books by the author**

*A New York Wedding – a novel*

*Bully Boss – a Novel*

*The Road Warrior – A sales manual*

*Advertising Copywriting*

*21 ½ Things You Need to Know Before You Self-publish*

*Study Guide for the US Immigration Test in English and Spanish plus Study Guides in 10 bilingual languages and a CD.*

My Website: http://www.swedenberg.com/

# Index

401k, **8, 24, 30,** 55

Amazon.com, **9,** 66

APR, **31**

APY, **20, 21**

**Auction, 45**

Bank account, **7**

Bar Rescue, **10**

Brokerage account, **8, 30, 64**

Brooklyn, **10, 13**

Cadillac, **36**

CarFax, **39**

CarsDirect.com, **45**

CD, **6, 9, 21, 23, 66**

Certified Financial Planner, **25**

Certified Pre Owned, **37**

Chevy, **35, 36, 38**

Chrysler, **35**

Consolidating debt, **62**

Danaher, **52**

DEA, **12**

Dividends, **8, 49, 52**

Division of Small Business, **18**

Edmunds, **31, 34**

Family Dollar Store, **52**

Fidelity Investments, **27**

Fitbit, **61**

Florida, **55**

Gap Insurance, **43**

Gene Autry, **1**

Google, **38, 58**

Gordon Ramsey, **10**

Greenville South Carolina, **1, 51**

Guarantees, **32**

Home Line of Equity, **62**

Hopalong Cassidy, **1, 2, 5**

Initial Public Offering, **52**

IRS, **55**

Janssen Pharmaceutica, **29**

Johnson & Johnson, **29**

Jon Taffer, **10**

Kitchen Nightmares, **10**

Long Island, **6, 27, 61**

Long-term capital gains, **64**

Marcus Lemonis, **10**

Mass Air Sensors, **63**

Mercedes Benz, **36**

Money, **iii, vii, 1, 3, 4, 5, 6, 7, 8, 9, 13, 14, 16, 17, 18, 20, 21, 23, 25, 26, 27, 28, 29, 30, 31, 37, 38, 39, 41, 42, 43, 44, 45, 47, 48, 49, 50, 51, 52, 54, 55, 57, 58, 61, 63, 65**

Money Market, **20, 21**

Mutual Fund, **20, 21, 22**

Mutual Funds, **9, 23, 24, 28, 52**

New York, **18, 28, 32, 51, 55, 61, 63, 66**

New York State Development, **18**

New York Times, **28**

Pizzeria, **13, 14, 15, 16, 17, 18, 19**

Pontiac, **33**

Principal, **4, 6, 8**

Procter & Gamble, **29**

Queens, **50**

Quickenloans, **58**

Roy Rogers, **1**

Rule of 72, **20, 23, 29**

Saab, **36, 44**

Short-term capital gain, **64**

Small Business Administration, **17**

**Smart Money, i, 8, 17, 20, 25, 30, 37, 42, 43**

Social Security, **8, 24, 25, 26**

Stock Broker, **25**

**Stupid Money, i, 6, 13, 24, 37, 42, 43, 45, 46, 54, 62**

SUV, **49**

Swedenberg Beer Garden, **10**

The Profit, **10**

Timeshare, **57**

Travelocity, **58, 59**

Volvo, **35, 36**

Wall Street, **51**

Warranty, **32, 33, 37, 40**

Woodhaven New York, **26**

Xerox, **52**

www.ingramcontent.com/pod-product-compliance
Lightning Source LLC
Chambersburg PA
CBHW061201180526
45170CB00002B/905